Shores and Headlands

Princeton Series of Contemporary Poets

For other books in the series, see page 82.

Shores and Headlands

Emily Grosholz

Princeton University Press

Copyright © 1988 by Princeton University Press
Published by Princeton University Press, 41 William Street,
Princeton, New Jersey 08540
In the United Kingdom: Princeton University Press,
Guildford, Surrey

Library of Congress Cataloging-in-Publication Data

Grosholz, Emily, 1950-
Shores and headlands / Emily Grosholz.
p. cm.—(Princeton series of contemporary poets)
ISBN 0-691-06749-X (alk. paper): ISBN 0-691-01448-5
(pbk.)
I. Title. II. Series.
PS3557.R567S5 1988
811'.54—dc19   88-5390 CIP

Publication of this book has been aided by a grant from the Lockert Fund of
Princeton University Press

This book has been composed in Linotron Bembo

Clothbound editions of Princeton University Press books
are printed on acid-free paper, and binding materials
are chosen for strength and durability.
Paperbacks, although satisfactory for personal collections,
are not usually suitable for library rebinding

Printed in the United States of America by
Princeton University Press,
Princeton, New Jersey

For Bob

Al cor gentil rempaira sempre amore
come l'ausello in selva a la verdura.

Contents

Acknowledgments   ix

Exchanges
The Gold Earrings   3
Exchanges   5
The End of Summer   8
Fausse Couche   10
Letter to Ruth from Durham   11
The Sycamores   14

Vagabondage
Siesta   19
Mediterranean   20
On a Line from Kavafis   21
The Old Fisherman   22
St-Germain   23
Raschplatzhochstrasse, Hannover   24
On the Untersberg, Salzburg   25

Exile
Letter from La Plata (I)   29
Interval   30
Letter from La Plata (II)   31
Exile   32
Letter from La Plata (III)   33
Theories of Vision   34
Letter from La Plata (IV)   37
The Carnival of Dreams   38
Two Variations on a Theme   39
The Purblind Letter   41
Summer Lightening   42

Italian Elegies
Sidelit   47
Via della Lungaretta 74   48
Beach Clubs at Ostia Lido   49
In the Abruzzi   51
The World as Will, Idea, *Grappa*, and Pigeons   53

Dialogue of Body and Soul   54
Another Song   56

Philosophers
The Return   59
The Warning   61
Perceptual Acquaintance   62
After Timaeus   63
Nietzsche in the Box of Straws   64

Prothalamia
The Outer Banks   71
Open Secrets   72
The Ratio of Green   73
The Courtyard Revisited   74
Moving   75
The Accident   76
Madonna mia, quel dì ch'Amor consente   78
The Tempest   79
The Cliffs at Praiano   81

Acknowledgments

The Hudson Review: Exile (eight parts), The Outer Banks, Open Secrets, The Courtyard Revisited, Moving, The Tempest, The Cliffs at Praiano

Prairie Schooner: In the Abruzzi, Via della Lungaretta 74, Dialogue of Body and Soul

Cumberland Poetry Review: St-Germain, Mediterranean, The Gold Earrings

Poetry: Siesta, The Old Fisherman

Southwest Review: On the Untersberg, Salzburg, The Purblind Letter

Kairos: After Timaeus, Perceptual Acquaintance

The Yale Review: The Warning

NER/BLQ: Summer Lightening

Michigan Quarterly Review: Two Variations on a Theme

Pequod: Nietzsche in the Box of Straws

Salmagundi: On a Line from Kavafis

Boulevard: Another Song

The author would like to thank the Djerassi Foundation and the National Humanities Center for their support, as well as her friends at *The Hudson Review*.

Exchanges

The Gold Earrings

I thought that I would meet you here.
You stood on the pavilion beside *Nepenthe*
where the view is still the same.
Nepenthe, you told me, means forgetfulness.
You reminded me to notice the body of earth
so often that our exchange
melts back into a hundred other occasions.
Surely we admired the cliffs together
descending and descending to the horizon
south of San Luis Obispo; singular pines;
the blue Pacific arrested in a motion
so vast and tranquil it resembles staying.
Forgetfulness pours through the enormous veins
that bind and furrow the world,
the ancient rivers of Acheron and Lethe.
Mother, souls who must begin again
drink at those deep channels; so I began
long ago the process of forgetting.
Not that memory grows less intense,
but the period of recollection lengthens.

I thought that I would meet you near
the lion-color mountains,
twisted cypresses weathered to silver
unchanged by twenty years, the cyclic ocean
enchanting and shaming thought into reflection.
Time came round full circle like the horizon
and placed us at the center
talking together, drunk with the blue of distance,
your voice clear as ever: pay attention
to the lovely body of earth. Nothing endures
in the end but the colored bones,
the mantling blood of ocean flowing down,
forgetfulness. No less intense, I swear,
just more infrequent as the years go by.

How body wears the mind in recollecting.
Tears blinded me at the door of *Souvenirs*,
where we chose a pair of long gold earrings
I loved and lost. The last I ever wore;
for later on, my taste in ornament changed,
and they were peerless, after their own kind.

Exchanges

I almost found you a car, *she said,*
driving me to the train in her husband's
Cadillac as sunset fired
gunpowder clouds above Long Island Sound.

My friend Dan died of emphysema.
I'd visit him in the hospital
every couple of days and sometimes
say, come on now, let me have the title.

Face it, why do you want a car?
I have another friend who needs
that car a lot. But he refused,
hoping, I guess, he'd get back on the road.

All alone. He had no people,
I was the only one to visit.
How did I meet him? *She paused*
at a stoplight melting into the red sunset.

When I started to fish, no one
would take a woman out in the boats.
I fished on the beach, loving to just
stand thigh-deep in waves, to cast and cast.

Still I wanted to try out deeper
water, go after bigger fry.
Finally someone told me to ask
Dan and he agreed, to my surprise.

He looked after me, not letting
any other fishermen
swear or throw their weight around.
"Watch your mouth when there's a lady present."

He was really . . . *She made a gesture*
of nothing between ear and ear.
Dumb. He was. But also more
careful than the rest of them, and kinder.

She threw one arm out in loving
extravagance accompanied
by a ghost-flourish of the plastic
cigarette holder she'd given up for good.

And he was a hell of a fisherman.
He thought like a fish. We'd putt
through acres of indifferent water,
suddenly he'd say *here* and then by god

I'd drop my line and pull them in.
He pretended he had money, though
once when he was sick, I saw
how much: his bankroll scrunched into a shoe.

His landlady let me in to find
his mail. I gave him money then,
out of my grocery budget, a hundred,
two hundred maybe; enough to pay the rent.

When he died, a niece suddenly
materialized with regrets and took
the little he left, including the car.
Then a lady called from Mamaroneck

who also wanted the car, claiming
he owed her; but she drew a blank.
He used to paint her houses. I think
she gave him money too and wanted it back.

In fact, the hospital official
who took his case post-mortem found
Social Security sent him nothing.
I have no idea what he lived on.

Sunset flagged and shivered in
the winter trees. She sighed, brushing
imagined ashes from her coat.
I don't like hospitals or visiting,

but I liked him so I went,
watched my friend adrift in bed.
So after all, my dear, I didn't
get your car, but you should know I tried.

The End of Summer

On Narragansett's littoral,
my brother checks the damage, starts
to set his lightly painted mussels
back to rights, around their bed
of mud and grass. What animal
walked over his experiments,
blind to the order it unmade?

Creatures of the tidal zone
are few, and manage their domain
as a refined cooperative:
so mussels make themselves at home
most readily where grasses weave
their archipelagos above
the variance of shore and sea.

"Federal funds, especially grants
pertaining to environment,
have presently become so scarce
we cannot offer at this time
the hope of a position here."
The sorry letters come as summer
and his research run to term.

He hears the deep disharmony
of speechless voices in the waves,
positioning his foot like Hermes
on the undistinguished mud;
counts his creatures one by one,
surprised how far his mollusks bear
their standards, yellow, red, and green.

Such rapid generations cross
his path, he wonders where a year
will find him, why his father lost

the wish to live, and disappeared.
Those mussels are not stay-at-homes,
sessile as barnacles, but spend
much of their lifetime to explore.

Before they have become too great
with age, they often hoist their threads,
anchor and mandarin whisker, pass
like curious magellans out
to sweeter, steadier terrain.
All this my brother verifies
in colorful geometry.

Dear spirit of inventiveness
and crossroads, parting of the ways,
if you can salvage your marine
a little from the muck of time,
uncertain future, vanished past,
then bring the gold proportion down
upon that other life, your own.

Fausse Couche

Without intentions, even
without the fine machinery
of sight, you looked away.
How riddling now our quiet
conversations seem,
that filled so many sunlit
autumn afternoons.
"Are you comfortable, and warm?
Are you there?" I took your silence
as natural affirmation.
"The sky is blue," I offered,
"the color your blood runs,
apples gold as your small
corporeal mind. The brambles
curve downward like a spine;
the silver willows lean
as we do in the wind.
If you are inches long,
with closed eyes and fingers,
perhaps you touch the edge
of your mother's vision."
But nobody attended:
only a little wind-egg
forgetting to multiply
despite all my descriptions
of quick cloud shadows
which, vanishing, kindle
the flanks of the low hills,
the violet woods, for eyes
still closed, I thought, for eyes
still deep in the great blindness
that stands before and after
our interval of light.

Letter to Ruth from Durham

Dear Ruth,

The lampshade latticed with amaryllis
you made from thread and parchment, reminiscence
of a round that we once practiced climbing a mountain
and sing whenever our paths cross again,
throws silhouettes of that twice-ghostly flower
beyond its own perimeter and pole
of glass jar filled with Carolina shells.
Life's small ironies. Your presence always
haunts me in this uncluttered southern city
where you computed flowers, started a family,
and left just months before I came myself.
The lamp lights up a corner of my life
on evenings when I return from watching stars
at their ordinary commerce through the coarse
headlands and inlets of loblolly pines
pitch-black against the paler stretch of sky.

Looking up encompasses vertigo.
Perception constructs its intricate rondeau
as it falls singing through those billion miles,
as light streams from the past, bending our wills
and eyebeams to self-limiting arabesques
Pascal commended and wise Leibniz sketched,
summing infinities in their quadrature.
And yet containment yields before a stronger
impulse to override all boundaries:
our cosmos radiates, diversifies,
and where are we, at its expansive heart?
You and I three thousand miles apart
in the universal diastole must share
a collocation. Tell me where we are,
if you still guide me through the glassed-in green
houses and labeled trails of local gardens.

Over the years, your offhand, patient lectures
have made these zones of dark and light converters,
with and without the extravagance of spines,
familiar country, closer, well-divined.
How you display the biography of boulders,
tapping open archaic fruit whose weathered
rind conceals morphosed or crystal flesh,
two hundred million years of sleepy ripeness:
so old their age embarrasses the mind
with ancestors it shudders to comprehend.
How you lift up the glossy leaf of ginger
to show its homely brown bell slowly rung
by a fertilizing beetle drunk on pollen,
or lead me to the early flowering jasmine,
or summon Hesperus winking like a pendant
along the ecliptic's true invisible chain.

Where are we, dear companion, looking down
at silent ancestral litter hung with garlands
chlorophyll, water, and energy invent;
looking up at stars equally ancient
whose future we were, whose past we become.
Adrift in two infinities, at home
in the world intelligence and loving fashion.
Perception offers rocks and stars, red fictions
shifting at the heart of constellations,
runnels of iron staining the carmine-brown
clay of the Carolinas. Inference
offers us its embodied, sensuous,
and therefore finite purchase on what always
calls and eludes us: the wild boundlessness
of nature in her wrack of times and spaces.
Affection integrates the differences.

You stayed here seven years, and went away
leaving the local pinewoods, gardens, sky
full of proper names, gentle instructions.
I've looked for that low field on the edge of town
you sowed for the odd ends of experiment,
counting its mint by thousands, measuring out
their least parameters for the axial ribbons
a computer ties on clusters of information.
And though I haven't found your field of mint
now surely run to seedy dissidence,
their scientific title has a power
charming enough to make this place familiar.
Salvia lyrata, like a spell,
conjures specifically your musical
and saving grace. So in the end I truly
find and miss you.

                        Love, from Emily.

The Sycamores

On the tenth anniversary of my mother's death, December 31, 1985

Home for the holidays but doubly homeless,
I drive around suburban roads in silence
thinking about the year past and its losses.
Tilting the new year forward:
possibilities stream like shapely light
in the angled mirror, raindrops on the windshield.

The old familiar outskirts of Philadelphia
I know like the veined and pale back of my hand.
Small valleys ranged on rivers,
eighteenth-century farms of somber fieldstone,
Victorian villages with borrowed names,
and shopping malls that sprout at the edge of fields.

Wondering where I've been and where I'm going,
I drive over forested ridges behind Paoli,
back across Newtown Square toward Villanova;
wherever I turn I see
the great white sycamores glittering together
in the slanted afternoon of winter solstice.

They open sheerly from their patchwork boles
into the purer white of upward branches,
the white of simple elements: marble stairs,
bones on the desert, freshly laundered linen,
the sheets my mother used to hang outside
to dry in winter sunlight.

And I'd go charging through
as if they were laminae of cloud. Oh lord,
how I want to go back home. As I slowly circle,
confounding the locations, driving and driving.

Partly I see and partly head out blind
on back roads starred by signs at intervals.

Attracted and repelled,
I'm like a particle skittering through fields
of memory arrayed as nested curves
on the warp of space where time comes round again.
Swerve to my mother's smile, the tended garden
sleeping in winter, all those lovely books.

The books my father hid behind at night
in our flawed domestic order. Quite imperfect,
but playful when my brothers first arrived
and my parents tried again,
and some nights left us children alone together
to racket around and stay up till all hours.

Veer away from the sadness.
Those dinners when my father watched the news
with nothing left to say, and my mother talked
incessantly as long as he didn't hear,
the odor of flat sex seeping across the kitchen.
Stronger than onions, even the children smelled it.

Then we grew sad and chilly. Afternoons
sometimes my mother took me and my brothers
(as if there were no father,
only a cold gray mist along the road)
to scatter our mid-winter ritual largesse
at a duck pond under a copse of sycamores.

How numbing the cold was, how hard the invention
of gaiety with two small abandoned boys
and a bitter woman. I never saw the trees.
So it seems strange today

to find them standing by the pond, neglected
by other families and flocks of birds.

Guardians, watchtowers, prophets of redemption.
They waited twenty years to shine again
in flamboyant ivory
the lonely traveler pauses to admire,
for whom at last their characters of light
describe a larger pattern on the sky.

Vagabondage

Siesta

Sphendouri, Aegina

All afternoon the heat intensifies
in leaps, like goats climbing the terraced hills;
another fig bursts on the tree; the olives
surrender another cache of livid shadow.
Cicadas transpose their note to a higher key.
As if the ear were the most material sense,
they sing us back to flesh and bone, the steep
rocky quarter acre where we happen to live.

But the eye is aethereal, that watches over
the tranquil cool Aegean, mantle of blue
woven east and west with the stitch of wind.
We see beyond our country into another,
familiar, never attained, where scattered islands
gather like the dream's immortal children.

Mediterranean

Where is Ardiaeus the Great?—PLATO, *The Republic*

Salt crystals in the hollows of limestone.
On a great, slanted rock I lay, like one
of the sea's translucent children, caught
and finished by the rain of light.
So close the world's incurable inversion
I saw the thorny stars far underwater,
anemone's dark rose the eye of Mars.

Wind from Africa tangling in the pines
wailed through its house of permanent exile,
Who has brought us here? I threw my bottle
of wine away, the sun drank me instead
as if I were forgetfulness. On the white verso
of cliffs, broom scored the tyrant wind
descending headlong like a soul in Plato.

On a Line from Kavafis

I never found them again,
those gold-flecked eyes,
thin limbs, a mouth too sensitive,

though I kept his addresses
and could have sent a letter,
forwarded, six months or a year later.

I never met him again,
but think of him with gold-stained hands
folded across his breast,
a satchel for his paints under his head,
asleep beside the sea at Aégina.

The eucalyptus have him now, not I,
orchards of blue pistachio,
almond trees, the windy olive groves.

The Old Fisherman

François Dejanna, d. 1980—L'Anse d'Orso, Corsica

He stands beside his ancient, lovely mistress
dreaming of silver fishes caught in the nets,
not of his dozen children, scattered to Calvi,
Ajaccio, who knows where; nor the somber Sunday
visits his wife still pays him, bringing provisions
to go with the bouillabaisse he concocts with lemon
or fennel and (always) a cork. He looks over his lines
woven from rosy silk, like her body at dawn.

Nothing remains this morning of his old passion
but a brace of fishes thrashing on the sand.
The horizon is firmly drawn, like a refusal
to settle with human folly. Cupped in his hand,
she etches its palm with salt, alone among all
the forgotten, whose violence answered to his own.

St-Germain

My bags are packed with magazines and scarves,
my cloudy head, my heart with memories
bitter and dry as half-smoked cigarettes,
flawless as a grocer's hill of peaches.
Finishing my coffee in an apartment
close to the bridge that crosses to the Louvre,
I think of Delacroix's Algerian women,
Titian's Venus with her dark-eyed mirror.

Paris behind me, through the open window
sunlight enters like the threat of love.
Occasional seagulls ride above the river,
dreaming as I do of the North Atlantic,
which I will shortly cross, bearing away,
dear thief and lover, all that I can carry.

Raschplatzhochstrasse, Hannover

The passages of exile I have read,
deciphering my own familiar hand,
run like a major artery between
the heart of yet another radiant town
and the long corpus of strange neighborhoods.
Thus on a rainy summer night I stood
suddenly motionless before a sign
that changed its green to red, its red to green.

I was afraid of the dark street, the gleam
transforming on wet asphalt, and the sigh
of planing cars with shrouded passengers.
Then it seemed possible to go back home.
How strangely hope allies itself with fear
and crosses over to the other side.

On the Untersberg, Salzburg

Another world, silent underneath the whine of wind,
the strange cries, like dry hinges, of the eagles,
thousands of bees droning across rock gardens'
embroidery on long grass, pasture after pasture,
peak beyond peak: edelweiss, gentian, anemone
weaving the summer habit of transhumance.
Shepherds lead their flocks up so many stairs
for these free riches, green to the line of snow.

Snow still rests in hollows like sheets of limestone,
but quicker, gone in a season, not an age;
darker rock is studded with ammonite and coral
left by a vanished ocean's vast reversal.
Silence gathers among the bonsai pines, knotted and corded
by wind. I hear the great stone ear curve toward me.

Exile

Letter from La Plata (I)

Blood sickens the air today.
It drifts from the pampas, from the cattleyards
out of the past to contaminate the future.
I fear the present uncertain compromise
of military and civil authority
will soon reverse itself
to pour a scarlet pest on all our houses.
So from this heartless south,
this paradise demons have won and lost,
I send my love with only a few words.
Perhaps my solitude, the dislocation
of Spanish into English, slow my voice.
Yet truly our conversation never ceases.
You are for me a diffuse and concrete presence
that circles in my blood,
revives in each fresh impulse of my breath.
I sleep for only a few hours at night,
teach all day and gather with my friends,
discussing strategy till early morning.
My children wait to see me on the weekends.
I miss you. Patience, distance, stoicism
are all I have to offer; my desire,
the shape of desire written on the air.

Interval

So are all Distances contracted in the Soul itself, and there Understood
Indistantly . . .—R. CUDWORTH, *The True Intellectual System of the Uni-
verse* (1678)

I saw the love-light first kindle your eye
in *Pupille*, a little bar in Saxony.
Philosophers' congress. Cold November rain
dissolved the window into constellations,
flocks and spirals of reflected streetlight.
Two days you dazzled me, then disappeared
like a star falling under the horizon.
Now at the center of the Southern Cross
you burn obscurely in my memory,
dark retina that repossesses heaven.
So as the sky's imagined hemisphere
is compassed by the pupil of the eye,
all distances contract within the soul
and there are understood indistantly.

Tonight again, a luminous cold rain.
There must be as much reality in the cause
as in the dear effects: so from your hand,
covering page after page of blue, I read
the true determinations of your heart;
and this autumnal weather writes again
your face across my eye's inverted glass.
We took each other with a sweet unreason
that crossed the boundaries of body and place.
For thought of a mile, of ten thousand miles,
even the semidiameter of earth,
takes up no greater room within the soul
than the short interval which parted us
that night, until you closed it with a kiss.

Letter from La Plata (II)

A poet in this country can only describe
the drama of uncertainty and loss
in an orphaned idiom,
a broken language without history.
Who listens to my verses? My dead friends?
My girls, imprisoned, tortured, or in exile?
The past has slowly disappeared behind me.
Today I write to you while drinking maté,
a kind of Indian tea favored by those
who are poor and mad. You see that I am both.
This government is like a drunk, vindictive
and unpredictable guardian
who sets up the rules one day
in order to countermand them on the next,
so all its baffled children are bound to err.
The latest news is that the agency
for research refused my work on Galileo.
Four hundred years of conceptual advance
mean nothing to those religious men, who find
in science only reason for suspicion.
(You notice, however, they don't mind buying arms,
the most contemptible and stupid offspring
of Galileo's great intelligence.)
"Blind Galileo, father of the moon."
I like the way your poem honors the past,
its bitter losses and his own
long stubborn recollection of the truth.

Exile

At the antipodes, where clouds of herons
darken the waves and fish circle in air,
where palm trees fall asleep, bury their branches
as if the heart of earth were another sun,
our winter is your summer. So you leave
the city, traveling south over the pampas
to where the unquiet waters of La Plata
melt into the sea's dark consolation.

Your small white house faces on the ocean.
Bougainvillea glitters on its walls,
viridian spangles and a private fear
staining your foreign journals, books and papers.
Perhaps the man next door, hired to survey
your various pursuits, will be surprised.
"Tell me, professor, yesterday afternoon,
who was that woman standing in the doorway?"

Sunlight angles through the vivid leaves.
She waits beside you in her light green dress
as if a winter rose opened in summer,
dream of a shadow, creature of a day.
You cannot see her. "No, I have no secrets,"
you answer. "Come and look. You were deceived
by the shadow of bougainvillea on the doorsill.
I live with that strange girl, my solitude."

Letter from La Plata (III)

I enclose two leaves from my dear ginkgo,
whose history is strange (and so, quite real).
Its parent tree arrived here from Japan
in 1882, an Emperor's gift
to celebrate the founding of La Plata,
and like a monument grows in the park
around the corner from my parents' house.
In fact, many Japanese have settled here,
and one of them, a friend,
promised me a bonsai from this ginkgo
upon the occasion of our hundred years.
At first it was a flawless little tree,
fragile and wise. But after a few seasons
I saw it grew too fast,
excessively, becoming a kind of dwarf
without a place in the great chain of being.
The more I watered it, the more it grew
ambiguous and all out of proportion.
Today I think of us, and of my tree.
For we are neither the simple artifice
of an affair, nor the natural expanse
of love with room to breathe,
foliage of such complexity and grace
it weaves a second sky. I mourn for us.

Theories of Vision

I.

Train the eye to see
colors long faded
from the marble throat
of Immortality;
colors past the sill
of our red and purple,
sheer embroidery
on petals of the white
violet, white rose.

Train the hand to draw
straight lines, circles
true as the simple
motions of the planets
and elements that fall,
so the empty brush
above white paper
traces to their source
rivers of the air.

The heart, impatient,
tangled in her lines
of stress, red traces
of dead or living passion,
must come to learn
with hand and eye
certain renunciations:
the brush run dry,
not sensual vision.

II.

Timid and fluid rainbows
over the nacreous surfaces
of shells, on peacock feathers

34

and soap-bubbles, appear
whenever incident light
reflects off nether and upper
laminae of films, one wave train
tagging after another
like a younger sister.

Destructive interference!
Which, for a given thickness
of film, only allows one color through.
So, on the peacock's wing,
here it is royal purple,
there it is blue:
quarrels of luminous children
crossing, of space and time,
the unending recess.

III.
On the lawn of trampled strawberry and clover,
your daughter blows across her plastic monocle
sending down a shower of bright bubbles,
rainbows clasping their selvages at every corner.

Rise, oh rise, she says, fantastic creatures,
though even she must see the midsummer air
is powerless to hold them, as the colors
drown, all the invisible hands let go at once.

IV.
Visible light goes in
the eye's black iris
(flowering at the margin
of a broad white river)
and never comes out again.
But absorbers are good emitters

and black is best,
so the eye also releases
(fresh circles on the river)
a different radiation
invisible to itself, that runs beyond
the roots of crimson, darker
than wine, or blood.

V.

Green leaves along the broken bough
drink sunlight, breathe our element.
We lose each other every night
but dream of the recurrences
that unexpected morning brings.
There is no other way of having,
so the red-lipped branches sing,
and our waking answers them.

So the scarlet voices chorus
as the world begins to fall.
Every longer evening brings us
home to supper by the fire
where the last light, slowly breaking,
fans its rainbow on the wall.

Letter from La Plata (IV)

No, I can't meet you anywhere right now.
Be patient with me, dear, never forget me.
I need the warmth and solace of your letters,
but Argentina holds me here
like a netted fish; my life is not my own.
You know I must still support
my parents, younger brother, and two children
on a salary inflation always reduces
to dust by the month's end.
Whenever I leave La Plata, my little girls
ask the same question: When will you come home,
papito, *come to live with us forever?*
And I stay on to teach philosophy
for my students, the young people, my own soul,
although my work is dangerously wounded
without the books I need.
Books! Those most desirable, necessary
creatures of the spirit, form and substance
of any innovation. They're never ordered;
sometimes they simply vanish in the mail.
Be patient if you can, and more clairvoyant,
as I so often see you on the street,
the broken pavement by my parents' house,
in darkened restaurants and crowded busses.
This difficult circumstance
allows no motive or strength for mere caprice.
I guard my love for you from hour to hour
just as I watch my children while they sleep.

The Carnival of Dreams

The ancient Greeks supposed
blood the seat and transport of our thought.
And so it seems, for midnight
brings you back embodied like a fever
though you were driven from my waking hours.

Those letters ceased, that brought
our endless talk across ten thousand miles,
the slow mail interjecting
weeks between each question and response,
time out of time. I guard the everyday,
surrender to my dreams.

So early morning greets me in confusion.
I stumble to the kitchen with your face
redoubling my vision,
hands still warm and fashioned to your body.
Let my cup of coffee be the charm
that chases you back to another country.

The carnival of dreams suspends
time in sweet illusory perfection,
focussing our spirits till they burn
like gunpowder roses, whiskey, memory,
gold flowers in the blood.

However often you come back again
to that bright labyrinth of tents,
you'll find me there.
Embrace the girl you see
three times; three times your open arms
will close across the incandescent air.

Two Variations on a Theme

Fare thee well oh honey fare thee well.—Dink's Blues

I.

Indian summer winds the trees
without recovering their ancient green
or leaving them in silence.
The enormous transience shimmers and burns,
beating its empty vans on the dry hills,
an old song caught in its throat.

One of these days, it won't be long . . .
Believe the song, my love, and not the singer.
Wild grape-vines string the lyre
of branches, bittersweet half-opens, ivy
glitters like the goddess's revenge
snaking through the forest, killing the boles.

So weather sings, and flowers
assume the claws of some fantastic creature.
Strange choirs out of season shake the air,
rapt in transmutation. *Call my name.*
Apples ripen inward, quinces
bruise like mottled hearts, black walnuts
tumble and litter the uncertain grass
that startles up, called by October's fictions.

Veronica follows the grass in all its errors
repeating the saviour's face,
each leaf with its bloody front and lonely gaze.
One of these days, it won't be long,
you call my name and I'll be gone.
The body of earth continues to decline
under the great, transparent shrouds of light.
Even gods are mortal. Trust the song.

II.
Light through the southern window throws
shadows of cedar boughs
and the ghost of a jay, who haunts their frail
shelter throughout the winter, on the wall.
Beyond the northern window, dusk
stains the hills to damask, then to plum,
sidelong to indigo. The leaves have fallen.
Sunset magnifies the neighbors' oak
to a system of borrowed light,
thousands of theorems drawn
from the bole's exhaustive axiom: I am.

If I had wings like Noah's dove
I'd fly down the river to the man I love.
But I stay here. Across the empty wall
autumn displays its passages in shadow,
re-creating the ancient masque
of emigrant light leading out all its flocks
along the Susquehanna, south
to Chesapeake and the ocean. Daylight drains
our darkened continent, and leaves a tree
of silver rivers read by satellite
whose eye revolves a thousand miles away.

Beyond the globe's meridian
spring is beginning on the underside:
tall grass fledges the pampas, passionflower
stares from balconies toward Ipanema,
ornament for the rich and shower
of inaccurate gaiety over the *favelas*.
The principles of light reverse themselves.
I am, I see, but only insofar
as I have been deceived.
Ambiguous delight withdraws behind
the window-screen, inflamed with visible night.

The Purblind Letter

The snow has finally stopped falling
from whatever lofty cerulean trapdoor
kept opening twice a day to dampen
the dumb exuberance of forsythia and bluet.
An inch of white slathering all horizontals,
rehearsals of color in the thaw and then
that damn visual silence. Enough white!
I need spring as a backdrop to write you
this long overdue and too-theatrical letter.

But, my love, you're almost impossible to address.
I talk strictly to God, myself, the sparrows,
the ghost of my wakeful father, long unburied,
lighting the four small chambers of my apartment,
diastole, dead white; systole, rose.
I see I've lost the knack of conjuring love.
All I got for months, my life, were dial tones
and busy signals, echoes of my voice
or the last apologies whispered by my father.

Now whenever I zero in, you vanish.
I wonder what coordinates I need
to run again into your strayed attention.
Don't fall apart like that, dear audible snow,
don't mute the little trumpets, poison
the tulip cups, leaving this late spring
triply intensified but fixed forever.
The bouquet of delicate corpses breathes, their stems
still pulsing, signing your name across my hands.

Summer Lightening

The blackberries are ripe. What good
does that do the abstracted girl
who skirts the woods, Brazilian jazz
trancing her mind, skittering down
the grounded streaks in her damp jeans?
Grasshoppers in their hundreds whirr
and lift, inverted ticker tape
to mourn, hurrah her thoroughfare
over the meadows as they fade.
One cheer for the summer *promeneuse*
just hitting middle age, dressed up
in a borrowed headset filling her ears
with jazz and the underscore of wasps,
mistaken in her heart's desire.
Mistakes leap scolding here and there.
How did they rise? Her heart perhaps
was green, unblown, a size too small,
not wishing the other well in all
his clarion ambiguity.
Too late, she picks her offering,
daisies with rain still in their cups,
the tilted wine of blackberries,
thinking, for god's sake, take them now.
The absent one reserves his right
to silence. She veers away again,
a careless rhythm in her gait.
Why not? Even the poor can count on
music, and even the bereft.
Willy nilly, the airs emerge
note-wise, unpaid for and unbidden.
She heads for the closely bundled sheaves
of goldenrod, fool's riches, good
for a sneeze and seven days of aerial
yellow scattered around the house;
and slows, unsettled by the sound

of distant surf breaking against Poros,
Monterey's brown harbor, coarsened
sea grass at the edge of Ipanema;
and wonders, staring at her hands,
how she can bear to bring these flowers home.

Italian Elegies

Sidelit

Slow shadows cross the Piazza Navone
and sudden storms of pigeons
all flying left, or right,
as the grip of some obscure obsession takes them.
Who lives on the terraces overhead
where nets of raffia weave through post and jasmine?
High-minded patricians, no doubt looking down
on swirls of us, importunate tourists
bent to our cameras like divining rods
for ice cream, wallets, snapshots, cut-rate shoes.
So I drift through the lengthening afternoon
thinking of musical D'Annunzio,
whom Croce detested for his lack of rigor.
How can passion weave itself through long
threads of analysis, the grid of meter?
Or how can it be uncoupled from obsession?
Passion turns one way, like Roman sunlight
gilding the low clouds of umbrella pines.
So I turn left, and left again
through sidelit labyrinths of streets
between the Tiber and the beautiful shell,
open to heaven, of the Pantheon.

Via della Lungaretta 74

Beyond the balcony, mechanics hammer
bashed-up carapaces, and grind off paint
from piebald Fiats with an electric blaster
that shivers and complains.
But here the creeping jasmine, fig and rose
in terra cotta basins, emerald lizards
who live on the walls' flat vertical, and I
with my feet in a pot of water, are very still.
We breathe the calm air of protected places.
Nobody knows we're here, except the neighbors
with right of access to other terraces
hidden in white ivy, who might look over
if they chose on our domain.
A radio throbs within the cavernous carworks
on the other side, sending up recurrent
wobbly jets of music, like a fountain
of mildly Arabic, four-four, five-four time.

I've been to the Capitoline, to view the pure
surreal of giant Constantine in pieces
propped in the courtyard of the left museum:
elbow, noble brow, a hand, some toes.
Along the galleries Michelangelo
designed to fasten broken antiquity
I noted the restraint
of marble poet and philosopher, the wolf
with her poised militant babies, and a pair
of beauties submitted to their makers' lust,
the Hellenistic boy drawing out a thorn,
and Caravaggio's Baptist. I have seen
more history today than I can bear.
Leave me to this garden then,
my feet in water and my head in flowers,
keeping my own counsel as the shadows
loom to the foreground like oblivion.

Beach Clubs at Ostia Lido

End of the line.
The Mediterranean Sea
framed by private entrances:
a brilliant likeness! Green
leaping just like water.
Why did I stop here?
The members hurry past
in families and pairs, not seeing
a girl in her elective
disaffinities. That must be I.

I won't pay for admittance.
Alone in the external
restaurant, dressed, dry,
I watch the swells:
breasts in their halters,
buttocks, mounded genitals
between such highly scalloped
triangles front and back
the swimming lovers
track each other openly.

The plane of sea
leans toward me, seethes.
Its violet horizon binds
the swollen, smaller world,
one of those alluring Genoese
maps, its coastal
margins lists of towns,
sea articulate with colored lines
in sixteen-pointed stars,
the winds' directions.

At the extremities, vast
desert places flower

with tents of Moorish kings.
How eros claims the explorers'
world. Is dream or error
the origin of passion?
Blow harder, winds, oh blow me
face to face at last
over those dark selves into the blind
alarming mirror.

In the Abruzzi

Two hours out of Rome, Celano
stands beside a vast invisible
lake which for unknown millenia ferried
sailboats and malaria.
A hundred years ago the new Italians
drained it; now only an oval plain
links the stranded villages
submerged in melancholy and fertile soil.

Switchbacks wander up to the *castello*,
whose crenelations flank
a courtyard squared by the slow repetition
of yellow gothic arches,
empty chambers fitted up with modern
radiator shells and casement windows.
I perched in one to overlook the lake
and dream of the wrong man.

Give the grapes a chance to bloom,
so green and bitter still, despite the season;
brush those wasps away from the ripe figs
they'd burrow in a day.
Let the cold wind quit the hills
and bring us summer fever unawares,
and send the stranger down. Or let him stay,
tell me his name, he looks so damn familiar.

Caro, sunlight falters in the shadows
of the unnatural palm trees which survive
harsh Abruzzi winters.
In passes between Torre and Celano,
carissimo, the snow will fly
before October ends on the gray slopes
above the ultimate pines, the bare unblessed
walls of San Clemente Casauria.

Like one of D'Annunzio's abandoned women,
the cloister lies in skeins of travertine
and fragments of the rose;
its vaults are empty, even the pigeons gone.
Caro, I think I see your face
in the squares of each provincial town.
This orphan passion fools me, since I never
send it away, or offer it a home.

The World as Will, Idea, *Grappa*, and Pigeons

Perhaps I've lost my sense of tragedy.
Oh pigeons who alight
one by one on the shrouded head of Bruno,
what have you known of life
in the Campo di Fiore, these many years?
As I sit measuring my ounce of *grappa*,
I size up passing Romans in my glass
and laugh at the comic wars
of love that stagger through my private opera.
The world has many crueller things to show.
Do I deserve a pigeon for a hat?
But every seventh man who passes by
takes on the aspect of my lost
beloved chiaroscuro,
multiplied, refracted uselessly
in the dazzle of broken shade.
A refill in my hand, I say
damn history's slow motion,
the tricks memory plays around my head.
Keep your distance, angels, curious pigeons,
I'm not a statue yet.

Dialogue of Body and Soul

Late in summer, the mistral overturns
the sea until its coldest layers
ride highest, chase the swimmers, chill
our Mediterranean colors.
Palm trees scythe the sun, cypresses
cease their perpetual incense, oleanders
shed their flowers in drifts of bitter rose.
Heaven becomes a hall of antique mirrors.

Frail impulsive body, everyday soul,
when we go out together hand in hand
even strangers suppose we must be lovers.
Strolling the boulevards,
we hardly dare to meet each other's eyes,
glancing at reflections in store windows.
We quarrel over details, the price of wine,
admission and hope, the lack of living space.

"Go back to your mother, then!"
"I can't, you know as well as I do
she's locked the door against me.
A grillwork of bone; nobody oversteps
that threshold. Where do you want me to sleep,
under bridges? In the arms of another soul?
Who'll keep me safe from the dispassion
of the mistral when it overturns the sea?"

We quarrel on the street, and even strangers
suppose we'll part someday.
Then it's tempting to envy the immortals.
Still, for all their fine despotic amours
flung across the sand like flowers of salt,
not one of them understands
the wisdom of our recurring argument
whose faulty logic proves it true.

Sailboats swerve and shimmer, disappear
along the blue of pathless memory.
We must have forgotten the ancient lullaby
that calls the sailor home:
Sweet and low, sweet and low,
wind of the western sea. Obscure,
steering our little boat like a single wing
in search of its other, what are we coming to?

Another Song

What do I want? A pair of espadrilles
that tie at the ankle; a kilo of white grapes;
a coffeepot that makes espresso upwards;
a bunch of lilies (gold and adder's tongue);
a lady's slip of hand-embroidered linen
to wear as a summer dress
with ivory bangles and a double belt
of Argentinean leather;
a studio with mirrors; a balcony
hidden in oleander; a little car
riding at anchor tethered to a street lamp.

What do I want? Nothing I don't have:
an hour to watch the ceiling of the sky
decorated by a hand
intemporal, figureless, purely expressive;
a sense of the absurd; another song.

Philosophers

The Return

The gesture of resignation
as the knight of faith
turns his hand like a calyx back
from the bloom on Isaac's cheek
shows that no illusion blunts his pain:
death lies on the rock.
Yet somehow Abraham regains
the life he laid aside: what floods
the empty circle of his arms?

The moon pulls back the waves
one by one from the sand,
lace covers quickly, hopelessly unmade
to yield the empty bed
of earth, the grave of love.
What radiance fills the place
from which the shining ocean fled?

The lover, lingering,
turns down the twisted sheet,
the last silk leaves of clothing,
hoping to see the other
shiver, warm at the root,
the blood flow back like summer.
But in the darker wake of love
each one restores the other, as they were:
here is your own, like Eve's
apple in hand. See, even the skin
is intact, with its luster and veins.

So the poet to her inventions,
so the mother to her child:
take, creature, your own true future,
its shape no longer moans and hides
in me, but wakes in you. And when that one
pulls on the globed
mantle of its own intentions,
what does the sad creator welcome then,
what rushes into the hollow of the heart?

Blind Galileo, father of the moon,
cheated of both telescope and eye,
what filled the dark horizons of your sight?
The dance of fire and stone
in order through the sky.

So the bereft, abandoned, blind,
cry to their lost inheritors,
go, you are not I.
The creatures flee and constitute the world;
the dance begins again,
the solid world, the moving world.
It is the world that enters in.

The Warning

Rhetoric's fairly planned
strategies for restoring
values often fall
foul in the event.
Historians recall
Cicero's tongue and hands
nailed to the Senate door.

What's the warning? Score
one for Caesar, one
for the translated Sophist.
Patroness of mutes,
a nightingale holds forth
on the Senate roof.
Her trill is ominous.

"Better speak than yield
to silence; and yet better
speak with your tongue
still fastened to your head.
Who needs more dead
eloquence, or tight-lipped
republican emperors?"

Perceptual Acquaintance

for John Yolton

An oak that bears ten thousand leaves
celebrates summer by my rented house;
clouds cover and display the sun.
Objective but not formal presences
enter directly the attentive mind.

They are in fact and always far away
as we walk underneath them, looking out
into the cloud of green, the leaving mist,
ten thousand swift appearances
which we, assembling, come to recognize.

They do not happen to us formally.
How could thought enclose a Japanese
garden, woven cloud and bonsai oak,
or open like the starry dome
with half of heaven really brought inside?

Neither in arrogance nor terror, turn
to the great external company
which we have never touched with hand or eye
and yet encompass with a fine
awareness that allows its own awareness.

Distance is grace; whatever fell
into the eye itself could not be seen.

After Timaeus

for Rémi Brague

The serpent is all belly, and Timaeus'
strange production nothing more at first
than radiant limbs about a living sphere
unconscious of itself, all ears and eyes
afloat in the matrix of the universe.

And what are we? Part snake, part crystal ball,
our hollow belly the low sounding board
where we first hear ourselves speaking or singing
and know we are the author of our song.

Sealed by the baleful birthmark of the navel,
we live with the necessity of evil
and breach our paradise, each time we fall
to speech, self-knowledge and the grand finale.

Nietzsche in the Box of Straws

What was real, in those days,
except our endless questions?
Except the eternal return
my love (who never knew
he was, all summer long)
so carefully expounded
on Saturday afternoons
to a group of curious students
in West Philadelphia, the year
I left, at seventeen,
my home in the green suburbs.
In front of my apartment
crowned by alanthus and dust,
a rosebush bloomed from June
to September; I go back
sometimes, to see if the crimson
roses are blooming still.
We broke for lunch at the Deli
around the corner, that sold
bagels and celery soda
we carried to the grounds
of the Catholic Seminary's
garden of rented plots.
Wild and civil flowers;
I'd stop by in the evenings,
lovesick, exhausted from
days at Horn & Hardardt's
and the rigor of argument.
One day we canceled class
in favor of the Zoo,
to see the hoary walrus
snorting, heaved on its side,
an oracle, if only
we had the ears to hear.
Oh, thou dry-footed, ghostly

children of the earth,
regret your frail, ill-fitted
and so inflexible spines,
learn from me the way
to be ponderous and fluid,
like the visionary prose
of Nietzsche, slipping under
the surface of the will's
abyss, its spiraled blue.
All week I carried trays
half-waiting, watching the door
for my dear philosopher.
Only the self-appointed
connoisseur who haunted
the gold limestone museum
came in for his cup of tea
late in the afternoon,
watching me bus dishes
like an animate caryatid
dressed up in ivory nylon.
Only Bessie, my colleague,
retarded, almost fifty,
whose heavy muscled arms
and awkward fortitude
reminded me of Popeye.
Only the Irish tyrant
who bossed us around the floor
and flirted with James, the cook,
who was easily half her age.
She watched us when we talked,
as I stood wrapping dozens
of triples of cutlery
in napkins, trying to read
my ragged copy of Nietzsche
stashed in a box of straws

at nose level. *Emily, what*
are you reading? Philosophy.
A German. *What does he say?*
He said, we always come
back to this very moment;
this moment will always happen
again and again and again,
as the universe combines
and recombines its atoms.
You believe that? If it means
we have to say to every
passing moment, stay,
be what you are, return,
I do. It's a discipline.
I see, he said; and he did.
Only our regulars
came through the revolving door,
claimed their usual tables,
unfolded the napkin, so,
aligned the silverware
and nursed their cup of coffee
until it was perfectly cold.
So the ingenious homeless
domesticate the most
improbable public spaces,
between the flyspecked walls
and naked, faceless ceiling
camouflaged by dangling
lamellate metal squares
in multitudes like silent
windchimes, while the Muzak
lulled us with its smooth
reductions of Bach and Rodgers.
Only the lost and hungry.
My dear philosopher

never appeared at my long
imaginary summons,
but came at the appointed
hour on the weekend.
So we talked in circles
around the constant center
of my recurrent dream:
he'd take me in his arms
and kiss me. Various, sweet,
unphilosophical kisses.
Suspended in the moment,
I'd answer, if indeed
that moment questioned me,
I see that you must pass;
by all the crooked pathways
skirting our finitude
that lead us out at last
into the limitless,
I look for your return.

Prothalamia

The Outer Banks

No ornaments but the double bed and open
solitude found in older motels off-season
with solid walls and purely anonymous cells.
Our bed was like a boat drawn up from the gray
Atlantic combing beyond our balcony;
the sound of breakers interwove in the fine
insistent pelt of rain that fell and fell
all weekend while we lingered, beached, protected,
under the sheets folded like canvas sails.

Sometimes we followed the usual path of tourists,
observing drifts of snow and Canada geese
settle into or lift off grassy marshes
through borrowed, diamonded binoculars
that brought them up so close they wavered on
our eye's own rushy edges, made precise
and flat by the forgetting of one dimension.
Flocks in your eye, my love, whole colonies
of gold sparks braving the darkened blue of iris.

We ran with our umbrellas pressed and flattened
like backwards feathers off the pervious wind.
Whenever the sun appeared at intervals
it scared up quarter rainbows in ones and pairs
out of the low bushes like quattrocento
angels. All things brushed across us then:
the braided strands, unbraided, of my hair
glancing your lips and cheek, and of your hands,
the touch that everywhere surprised my own.

Open Secrets

What can I tell of gratified desire,
the body's best kept secret? Open where
passion divides our streams of consciousness
and love, inspired, stormy, uncommanded,
seines the recursive tide.
Where you stand, naked as summer,
half-absorbed in the conventional labor
of rinsing coffee cups clear of their rimmed
cream at midnight, while I rearrange
mattress and sofa cushions on the floor
in imitation of the double bed
I lack. You are the heart of my invention.

Secrets of unexpected, slow transparence.
How love sets certain daily passages
of fine print in italics,
squares the odd capital in scrolling gold.
Beside your morning cup of Grand Souchang
surpassed by a traveling light and quenched
by clouds of milk, your hands
move thoughtfully about unconscious tasks.
I watch them lift the silver, ruffle a book
in search of fugitive pleasure, and recall
their spelling of my soul
so many times embodied, here and here.

The Ratio of Green

Among the colors, green, which consists in the most moderate action (which, by analogy, one can speak of as a ratio of 1 to 2), is like the octave among musical consonances or like bread among the food that one eats.—DESCARTES, *Treatise on Man*

Among the colors, green, we are the sudden
unexpected but undeniable
razzle of new grass on the fairways, hidden
by a bristling copse of southern pine and maple
behind our rented house. We lie protected
by so many velvet links from the emptying artery
of dark red highway, bloodied with sheer speed.

Our green is sudden but slow, the unlikely
but inevitable offspring of long sleep, revival,
and then blind inches by inches spiraling
through earth's brown leafy curls until the octave
rings openly in air, so its vibration
moves outward as impalpable spheres, as heavens
raised above the players' lowered ken.

Still half-asleep they linger, listening,
as if they merely respected the ninety-degree rule
but, slipped from the embrace of that expanding
music now translated higher, feel
their loss as satisfaction with the green
burgeoning underfoot, and walk away still
slightly dizzy, ears ringing, looking down.

Then we get up together, conjuring loaves
of bread for our breakfast table in plain air.
Analogy makes us the ratio of one
to two: two by virtue of separate stations,
one by virtue of music, a common color
woven like memory through our conversation.
The clear relation of one to two is love.

The Courtyard Revisited

Sometimes I only want to go underground
down my soul's obscurer steps, to the gate
not guarded by Cerberus but by the minor
bureaucrats of the Paris Métro, taking
the diagonal subway back in the direction
Mairie des Lilas, where I used to stay
in a courtyard now reduced to rubble, blocks
of concrete haunted by ghosts of lilac and maple.

Not to meet old friends, love, but to find
you waiting in one of the possible small houses
and live there alone together for weeks on end
unoccupied by any tasks but dreaming,
reading and writing thoughts on scraps of paper,
walking the streets in evening light that lingers
till ten or eleven, running a few last errands
and then returning to cook our supper late.

Hidden away in that courtyard where no one comes
but memory, I want to lie beside you
in a bed by an open window, listening
to swallows flying home as darkness falls
with the infinite slowness of northern summer evenings,
holding your lovely body, tracing its curves
in the gathering blue obscurity and singing
quietly songs known only to you and me.

Moving

Summer night drifts through the open door,
premature nostalgia lacing the wrack
of honeysuckle, pine and vagrant wings.
The walls are bare, all our possessions packed
in last week's news. We're leaving the red soil
and clement seasons of North Carolina,
the place where we began. For once I've learned
to trust in a beginning, reckon the gain
and count the loss as loss. Yesterday squarely
stowed away transforms our common future.

Somewhere north we'll find another house,
decorate its rooms with books' and voices'
invisible extension. Let our pictures
mirror us enframed by the back country.
Then whenever snow obscures the air,
we can see ourselves in the unchanging
green of southern pinewoods left behind.
Catch, my love, the evening's raffish perfume,
rumor of butterflies pressed to the scrim
of memory, still willing to tumble in.

The Accident

What happened at that moment? The world ended
then started up again like the slow heart
of a chick, exhausted, half-trapped in its shell,
a crazy star of blue showing overhead
where freedom lies. And yet the hard white walls
curve in and sideways like necessity.

What happened next? I didn't see, I turned
back minutes later, wondering what fate
had made my love so slow in caravan.
A flat tire, maybe. Oh, no. There were lights
flashing and his new car piled upside down.
The universe suddenly crumpled on itself.

I stood on the periphery and howled
till someone shook me. Stop it. I could hear
a voice: go quickly, hold your husband's hand
and talk him out of his dream. I found my love
somehow alive, and over a long hour
we weighed his version of the world and mine.

Mine was appalling, but less insubstantial,
so we concluded sadly, as we touched
across the broken glass, the frozen door.
Firemen cut him from the car with axes,
carried him gently into the ambulance
where all at once we felt how cold we'd grown.

The scenery whipped past us, bleeding shapes
and colors on the winter air. All day
hospital doctors searched him with the strange
blind eyes of radiation: he was sound
if all the tests were true. But in the evening
pain moved across his face instead of sleep,

then waves of morphine, then my hand's caress
that shivered with its inability.
Oh how the careless world turns off and on,
yawns and snaps like jaws, a half-crazed shell,
mysterious pale sedan cresting a hill
headlong in the wrong lane to stop my love . . .

We told the story many times, but faltered
just in the middle where the dark part came
that had no luck or motives. No good reason,
not any reason at all. And then we fell
silent together, uncertain of the tale,
hands touching through the bed's protective bars.

Madonna mia, quel dì ch'Amor consente

Madonna mia, quel dì ch'Amor consente
ch'i' cangi core, volere, o maniera
o ch'altra donna mi sia più piacente,
tornerà l'acqua in su d'ogni riviera,
il cieco vederà, 'l muto parlente,
ed ogni cosa grave fia leggera:
sì forte punto d'amore e possente,
fu 'l giorno ch'io vi vidi a la 'mprimiera.
E questo posso dire in veritate:
ch'Amore e stella fermaron volere
ch'io fosse vostro, ed hanlo giudicato;
e se da stell è dato, non crediate
ch'altra cosa mi possa mai piacere,
se Dio non rompe in ciel ciò c'ha firmato.

Guido Guinizelli

My love, the day love allows
change in my heart, will, or ways,
or that another please me more,
rivers must revert to source,
the blind see, mutes discourse,
earth like air or fire rise.
So decisive that day was
when you first lit my eyes.
As nature's truth I say this:
love and stars firmly attest
I'm yours. By common judgment,
heaven claims that no one else
can please my soul, unless
God crack the vault of heaven.

The Tempest

At last we climbed Michelangelo's Piazzale
to command the elaborate vista Arno divides
and bounds: intaglia of terra cotta
or copper green pressed on the plains, and flanks
of the tangent mountains.

Above us, not that cobalt Italian sky
whose formal self-effacement frames and phrases,
but weltering clouds. It never rains in Florence
this time of year, but dictum's overwhelmed
by soft appearance.

Humid, warmed, the air grew up around us,
thick citronelle of linden trees in bloom.
The perfume's German, and its arias
of hushing leaves and muted summer thunder
hauntingly northern.

Lost in one of those quarrels nobody wants
but history can generate as crossings
of long entangled lifelines, we sat down
in the lee of a cafe terrace, half-protected,
half-drenched by rain.

What else could we do but watch the tournaments
of cloud? They wheeled on Brunelleschi's Dome
fixed as invariant under transformation,
but meant to be seen against the wider flawless
blue dome of sky.

For us its red tiles wavered, slowly fused
like a stain on the winding currents of atmosphere.
The tears in things dissolve geometry.
So we observed by words, and the warming touch
of lips and hands.

Daisies massed on the terrace drank the rain.
Later, an intermittent beam of sunlight
broached the dusk and moved along the hills,
its path the fairest analogue we have
to a perfect line.

And yet how randomly the caressing light
wandered across the quartered town and vineyards,
planting its golden blotch on the linden trees,
our cafe's raffia arbors, and the curves
of the glinting river.

The Cliffs at Praiano

Remembering backwards, I foresaw you years
and years ago, in this lush obvious haven
for romantics, fishermen, homeless African wind.
West of Amalfi, east of Positano.
Our village curves to the sea in flights of stairs
suspended above the beach a few small
fishing boats, a clutch of swimmers, fill.
Whenever you enter our wide-angled, sultry
hotel room perched on the cliffs, or call
my name from the balcony, your presence shimmers
like a memory of great anticipation.

Every paradox religion loves
seems true as the hour opens on itself
and we fall through, into that numberless
and unexampled matrix. As the light
steps back across the cliffs and one by one
renounces the olive trees, the limestone
shelves, the Saracen fortresses, the pines.
How else could god, uncertain at the cross
of history, appear for us except
at a given hour, and how else could I touch
our love except in these particulars?

We have been happy in a truckstop south
of Roanoke, where shadows of semis loomed
across the windows, browning the yellow neon.
Love can do without the props of romance.
And yet Praiano moves us with its wild
theatrical display of elements:
headlands, currents, breezes, strands of light.
Look at the cliffs, I say, and mean instead
that you are irrevocable. Reflected
sea-light gleams on cliffs day has abandoned
just as you stand before me, in my words.

Princeton Series of Contemporary Poets

Returning Your Call, by Leonard Nathan
Sadness And Happiness, by Robert Pinsky
Burn Down the Icons, by Grace Schulman
Reservations, by James Richardson
The Double Witness, by Ben Belitt
Night Talk and Other Poems, by Richard Pevear
Listeners at the Breathing Place, by Gary Miranda
The Power to Change Geography, by Diana Ó Hehir
An Explanation of America, by Robert Pinsky
Signs and Wonders, by Carl Dennis
Walking Four Ways in the Wind, by John Allman
Hybrids of Plants and of Ghosts, by Jorie Graham
Movable Islands, by Debora Greger
Yellow Stars and Ice, by Susan Stewart
The Explanations of Light, by Pattiann Rogers
A Woman Under the Surface, by Alicia Ostriker
Visiting Rites, by Phyllis Janowitz
An Apology for Loving the Old Hymns, by Jordan Smith
Erosion, by Jorie Graham
Grace Period, by Gary Miranda
In the Absence of Horses, by Vicki Hearne
Whinny Moor Crossing, by Judith Moffett
The Late Wisconsin Spring, by John Koethe
A Drink at the Mirage, by Michael J. Rosen
Blessing, by Christopher Jane Corkery
The New World, by Frederick Turner
And, by Debora Greger
The Tradition, by A. F. Moritz
An Alternative to Speech, by David Lehman
Before Recollection, by Ann Lauterbach
Armenian Papers: Poems 1954-1984, by Harry Mathews
Selected Poems of Jay Wright, edited by Robert B. Stepto,
    Afterword by Harold Bloom
River Writing: An Eno Journal, by James Applewhite
The Way Down, by John Burt
Wall to Wall Speaks, by David Mus